Aspiring Affirmations

Intentional Connection for Couples

Jill Guzman

Copyright © 2024 by Jill Guzman

All rights reserved. This book or any portion thereof may not be reproduced or used in any manner without the express written permission of the publisher except for the use of brief quotations in a book review.

ISBN hardcover: 979-8-9901543-2-2
ISBN paperback: 979-8-9901543-0-8
ISBN ebook: 979-8-9901543-1-5

Design and publishing assistance by The Happy Self-Publisher.

Finally Time Publishing LLC

Dedication

For my amazing husband, Alex —
My partner, beloved, and friend...
My everything, my world.
Every day, more and more,
I love you like never before.

Table of Contents

Who Is This Book For? 8

What Are Affirmations? 10

What Does Aspiring Really Mean? 12

How To Use This Book? 14

Affirmations 17

About The Author 124

Affirmations

Authenticity	19	Nurturing	45
Balance	21	Openness	47
Connection	23	Peace	49
Devotion	25	Quality	51
Evolution	27	Respect	53
Friendship	29	Security	55
Gratitude	31	Tenderness	57
Honor	33	Unity	59
Intention	35	Validate	61
Joy	37	Willing	63
Kindness	39	eXploration	65
Love	41	Yielding	67
Mindfulness	43	Zest	69

Affirmations

Attention 71	Natural 97
Beauty 73	Optimism 99
Calm 75	Patience 101
Desire 77	Quiet 103
Ease 79	Rooted 105
Forgiveness 81	Support 107
Greatness 83	Trust 109
Happiness 85	Uplift 111
Intimacy 87	Value 113
Journey 89	Wisdom 115
Kinship 91	eXample 117
Loyalty 93	Youthful 119
Motivation 95	Zen 121

Who Is This Book For?

Hello and welcome! This collection of affirmations came about after I began looking for simple, inspirational, daily readings for my marriage. I was interested in finding positive, secular writings meant to be read aloud by two people in a committed relationship. All I found was an abundance of devotionals for traditional, religious marriages and a mixture of material for couples, from date night games to counseling journals and workbooks. Further research online revealed articles with simple couple affirmations, but they were mostly written from a singular perspective rather than a collective viewpoint.

Unable to find exactly what I was looking for, I decided to create my own. I initially wrote these affirmations for the sole purpose of reading them daily with my husband. They have been such a great source of intentional connection for us that I wanted to share them in the hope of inspiring the same for others.

This book is intended to be so broad and inclusive that truly any committed, loving couple can benefit from reading and applying these universal affirmations. Regardless of age, spirituality, background, or lifestyle, and whether you are in a serious dating relationship, engaged, newly wed, or celebrating many years within a committed partnership, I genuinely hope this heartfelt book encourages and uplifts all couples who open its pages. The only requirement is the desire to devote a few minutes with each other to grow together in love. Using these Aspiring Affirmations as your guide, my wish is for your relationship to deepen, creating more space to experience a connection full of intention.

What Are Affirmations?

Affirmations are made up of inspiring, motivational words, usually spoken aloud, that bring about a more positive perspective by shifting patterns of thought. An example of a simple affirmation may be: I am loved, or I am happy. They can be factual statements already in existence or what one wishes existed or had more of in their life. They are reminders and reassurances of our dreams, goals, and desires.

Affirmative language is recited consistently and repetitively because our brains remember what we regularly say to ourselves and what we do often. There is comfort in the consistency and familiarity in the repetition, ensuring that positive statements manifest within the mind as absolute truth.

Affirmations are generally written for individuals, but when voiced purposefully as a couple, both partners are actively working together to better themselves and their relationship. In reading inspirational, positive, loving statements as if they are facts, they become a core part of the partnership's belief system, naturally intensifying the positivity and love that already exists.

Spending time as a couple reciting these Aspiring Affirmations together, as a practice to prevent pitfalls, maintain milestones, and celebrate new accomplishments, can lead to a stronger bond and a more intentionally connected relationship.

What Does Aspiring Really Mean?

Aspiring can be defined as a strong desire or wish accompanied by a passionate, wholehearted effort to change and grow. Most affirmations are intended to be aspirational, but when utilized for romantic partnerships, the word takes on a deeper, more intimate meaning. Although intimacy is usually equated with physical or sexual actions, couples can connect through continuously recited affirmations that do, indeed, positively affect the strength of their bond.

There are five main types of intimacy: spiritual, physical, intellectual, recreational, and emotional. Being mindful of these relationship areas creates an ongoing gauge to measure and assess your partner connection. To make it easier to remember, I came up with an acronym I think is perfect: *A-S-P-I-R-E*. My husband and I, and hopefully all committed couples, are:

Aspiring
Spiritually
Physically
Intellectually
Recreationally
Emotionally

The acronym, which can be both a grounding point and compass for your partnership, truly brought this book of Aspiring Affirmations to life. Each affirmation contains an aspirational reminder to consider all areas of intimacy as you focus intention into your couple connection.

How To Use This Book?

Implementing an affirming practice for couples requires little effort other than an intention to connect with your partner. The process is easy, and takes just a few minutes of reading together.

Inside this book are fifty-two aspirational words and corresponding affirmations. The affirmations all consist of five uniquely written, yet structurally repeated sentences, designed to develop the simple practice of infusing positivity into your relationship.

How you choose to read and apply each affirmation is based on your comfort levels and preferences. You can read them alphabetically, randomly turn to a page, select words from the Table of Contents that resonate with you and your partner on a particular day, or focus on one affirmation at a time and review it daily for a week, repeating the cycle annually.

Experiment with who reads the affirmations and at what time of day, and remember to enjoy the process. The affirmations, although short and sweet, are meant to be contemplated and not rushed, so linger leisurely on the words as you and your partner engage in this planned activity. The goal is to give yourselves time to develop and take action with the words you are sharing. When two people come together as a couple with a common, mindful purpose to actively use these Aspiring Affirmations, the result will always be a stronger, deeper relationship built on intentional connection.

Happy Partnering...

We intentionally connect with each other to reach our aspirations of authenticity. We reveal our true nature to one another, knowing we are loved for who we are. We share wholly with honesty and accept our partner without judgment. We are free to fully be ourselves. We are authentic.

We intentionally connect with each other to reach our aspirations of balance. We focus on self-care and couple-care to maintain a steady state. We are aware of our inner and outer worlds, and adjust accordingly to create ongoing stability within our relationship. We are in equilibrium. We are balanced.

We intentionally connect with each other
to reach our aspirations of connection.
We both sense the unexplained energy
that links us together. We are each other's
person, and our hearts and souls are joined
in an unbreakable bond. We are eternally
bound to one another within this partnership.
We are connected.

We intentionally connect with each other to reach our aspirations of devotion. We are committed to the importance of our union. We share a steadfast loyalty to the other, expressing both adoration and admiration. We are dedicated to our partner.
We are devoted.

We intentionally connect with each other to reach our aspirations of evolution. We are an ever-expanding couple on a forward-moving path. We choose to better ourselves daily, aiming to consistently become the highest and best version of us. We are always growing. We are evolving.

We intentionally connect with each other to reach our aspirations of friendship. We truly like each other and enjoy spending time together. We are intimate companions and confidantes, freely sharing and receiving our thoughts and feelings. We are one another's beloved life partner. We are best friends.

We intentionally connect with each other to reach our aspirations of gratitude. We are thankful for our partner's contributions to our relationship. We show appreciation for who the other is and how their presence positively impacts us. We are so happy to share this life together. We are grateful.

We intentionally connect with each
other to reach our aspirations of honor.
We move through life together with integrity,
rooted in the purest of principles. We hold
ourselves to the highest of standards and
have the utmost regard for one another. We
respect our partnership. We are honorable.

We intentionally connect with each other to reach our aspirations of intention. We are a team full of dreams, diligently striving and working toward the well-being of our relationship. We align our ambitions to ensure they are complementary. We share a purposeful life plan. We are intentional.

We intentionally connect with each other to reach our aspirations of joy. We experience the beauty that is within us and all around us, and together we delight in our many blessings. We are peacefully content, having fun and enjoying all our life has to offer. We are filled with happiness and bliss. We are joyful.

We intentionally connect with each other to reach our aspirations of kindness. We calmly communicate with one another using thoughtful words and gentle gestures. We express ourselves with understanding, consideration, and courtesy, so our tenderness is felt. We are caring partners. We are kind.

We intentionally connect with each other to reach our aspirations of love. We experience and convey our deep feelings of passion, affection, and fondness for one another. We share a special bond, built out of romantic warmth and sweet endearment. We fully and thoroughly adore one another. We are in love.

We intentionally connect with each other to reach our aspirations of mindfulness. We openly observe our thoughts and feelings, allowing them to unfold freely and naturally. We are both self-aware and aware of each other. We are alert and focused on the present moment together. We are mindful.

We intentionally connect with each other to reach our aspirations of nurturing. We cultivate our relationship by supporting one another's growth. We bolster our partner and offer encouragement to attain our goals and dreams. We gently promote and foster each other's development. We are nurtured.

We intentionally connect with each other
to reach our aspirations of openness.
We choose to be vulnerable, sharing our
innermost thoughts and feelings with one
another. We are flexible, approachable, and
warm, creating a safe space for our partner.
We are receptive to each other.
We are open.

We intentionally connect with each other to reach our aspirations of peace. We purposefully infuse our relationship with calmness, tranquility, and ease. We work to consistently create and sustain a sense of serenity through mutual cooperation and collaboration. We are compatible and in harmony. We are at peace.

We intentionally connect with each other to reach our aspirations of quality. We ensure an upright relationship by implementing our shared foundational principles. We strive for excellence of character to be worthy of one another. We are ideal partners by being the best versions of ourselves.

We are of the highest quality.

We intentionally connect with each other to reach our aspirations of respect. We treat one another with courtesy and as an equal counterpart to ourselves. We easily recognize the other's value, regularly expressing our genuine admiration. We consider our partner with the utmost regard. We are respected.

We intentionally connect with each other to reach our aspirations of security. We feel safe and protected with our partner and within our relationship. We each maintain a presence of dependability and strength, reinforcing the sense of trust and confidence between us. We feel assured.
We are secure.

We intentionally connect with each other to reach our aspirations of tenderness. We have soft hearts for one another and approach our partner filled with goodness. We treat each other gently and with absolute kindness. We are benevolent and compassionate. We are tender.

We intentionally connect with each other to reach our aspirations of unity. We are two people joined together, living our lives harmoniously integrated. We embody oneness and wholeness, as a blended example of compatibility and agreeableness. We are an undivided, cohesive couple in unison. We are united.

We intentionally connect with each other to reach our aspirations of validation. We communicate with empathy to create a safe haven for sharing our thoughts and feelings. We are compassionate listeners, emotionally and mentally present for one another. We are seen, heard, and understood. We are validated.

We intentionally connect with each other
to reach our aspirations of willingness.
We bring a sense of eagerness to our
relationship, ready without hesitation, to be
present for one another. We are prepared
to be actively participating partners. We are
motivated and enthusiastic.
We are willing.

We intentionally connect with each other to reach our aspirations of exploration. We are a team on a path of discovery and seeking. We endeavor to learn and grow while choosing to invest our time as a couple into new and interesting experiences. We are journeying together. We are exploring.

We intentionally connect with each other to reach our aspirations of yielding. We choose to be receptive and open to one another's needs and viewpoints. We are humble and easygoing, able to freely and gladly accommodate and compromise when appropriate. We are flexible partners.
We are yielding.

We intentionally connect with each other to reach our aspirations of zest. We feel great passion for our partner and are both equally elated to be in this relationship. We experience enthusiasm and excitement simply because we are together. We truly appreciate the energy we share.
We are full of zest.

We intentionally connect with each other to reach our aspirations of attention. We consistently take notice of one another and regard our partner with the utmost importance. We show consideration and express warm concern for each other. We are aware and present partners.
We are attentive.

We intentionally connect with each other to reach our aspirations of beauty. We see and appreciate the wonderful internal and external attributes of our partner. We also have a special bond that goes beyond traits and attractiveness. We share an indescribable brilliance between us.
We are beautiful.

We intentionally connect with each other
to reach our aspirations of calmness.
We choose to create an environment of
mental and emotional tranquility within
our relationship. We experience a sense
of harmony between us and a sustained
peacefulness toward one another. We have
a serene partnership. We are calm.

We intentionally connect with each other to reach our aspirations of desire. We have similar goals for ourselves and each other, longing for shared life dreams. We also express passion for our partner, wanting to be intimate in all ways. We yearn to experience life completely with one another. We are desired.

We intentionally connect with each other
to reach our aspirations of ease. We
share a beautiful bond that is natural and
effortless, based on our mutual openness.
We experience a contentment within our
relationship that is filled with calming
comfort. We are both relaxed.
We are at ease.

We intentionally connect with each other to reach our aspirations of forgiveness. We show and communicate with compassion to both ourselves and our partner. We express hurts with patience and missteps with accountability. We choose to offer and accept apologies graciously.

We are forgiven.

We intentionally connect with each other to reach our aspirations of greatness. We are skillful masters of our relationship, striving to achieve the highest quality connection. We work hard to continually perfect the goodness between us. We are an amazing couple. We are great.

We intentionally connect with each other to reach our aspirations of happiness. We experience and express utter delight in sharing our lives together. We feel elated within our relationship and are filled with a sense of well-being and bliss. We are glad and joyful. We are happy.

We intentionally connect with each other to reach our aspirations of intimacy. We engage purposefully in behaviors that enhance our togetherness and deepen our connection. We are companions and lovers who experience a true sense of belonging. We share a closeness with our partner like no other. We are intimate.

We intentionally connect with each other to reach our aspirations of journeying. We see life as a process of progress, lifelong learning, and shared moments. We travel this path together in a quest full of forward moving experiences. We navigate each day with the other by our side.
We are on a journey.

We intentionally connect with each other to reach our aspirations of kinship. We represent the purest form of a relationship and are beyond proud to say we are family. We are near and dear to each other's hearts, sharing a unique closeness with no comparison. We are one another's person. We are kin.

We intentionally connect with each other to reach our aspirations of loyalty. We are completely faithful and utterly devoted to each other. We are tried-and-true partners, proving our trustworthiness with consistency and emotional support. We are dependable, steady, and reliable. We are loyal.

We intentionally connect with each other to reach our aspirations of motivation. We approach one another with enthusiasm and nothing but positive intentions for our relationship. We share an absolute willingness to continuously show up for one another. We are inspired by and for our partner. We are motivated.

We intentionally connect with each other to reach our aspirations of naturalness. We have the highest sense of familiarity with our partner, feeling comfortable and relaxed with one another. We are sincerely authentic and share the innate ability to simply be ourselves. We are both genuine.
We are natural.

We intentionally connect with each other to reach our aspirations of optimism. We are upbeat, happy, and confident as we go through life together. We enthusiastically see the bright side of situations, aware that our relationship is full of promise and potential. We are positive and hopeful. We are optimistic.

We intentionally connect with each other to reach our aspirations of patience. We communicate with our partner using gentleness and understanding. We offer time and space when needed to ensure our interactions remain both productive and loving. We calmly respond rather than react. We are patient.

We intentionally connect with each other
to reach our aspirations of quietness.
We desire and seek serenity within our
relationship and find it together with
purposeful nonaction. We enjoy peace and
tranquility in actively choosing relaxation
and stillness. We experience silence.
We are quiet.

We intentionally connect with each other to reach our aspirations of rootedness. We have established a stable and secure foundation with a fixed sense of togetherness. We continue to create our own history and have found a home in one another. We center and anchor our partner. We are rooted.

Support

We intentionally connect with each other to reach our aspirations of support. We provide comfort with compassion and kindness while showing our concern with respect and understanding. We can rely on each other to offer guidance and reassurance. We are a rock for our partner. We are supportive.

We intentionally connect with each other to reach our aspirations of trust. We give each other a sense of ultimate confidence through the constancy of our actions and words. We believe in each other and ensure our dependability with consistent behavior. We are reliable partners. We are trusted.

We intentionally connect with each other to reach our aspirations of upliftedness. We both choose to be an inspiration for the other, making our relationship lighter and brighter. We strive to enhance and improve ourselves in order to bring joy to our partner's life. We are energizing and upbeat. We are uplifting.

We intentionally connect with each other to reach our aspirations of value. We easily recognize one another's worth and vital contributions within our relationship. We readily express appreciation for the other and cherish all that we are building together. We are treasured partners. We are valued.

We intentionally connect with each other to reach our aspirations of wisdom. We move through life and approach our relationship intelligently, using reason and rationale. We continue to learn and discern, sensibly and soundly. We are grounded in knowledge and good judgment. We are wise.

We intentionally connect with each other to reach our aspirations of being an example. We work hard at our relationship to be models of excellence and goodness. We humbly shine our connection into the world as an inspiration for others. We are an exceptionally wonderful couple.
We are an ideal example.

We intentionally connect with each other to reach our aspirations of youthfulness. We are fun-loving, active, and full of life. We share our joyful and lively spirits with one another and express pure happiness to be in our relationship. We are vibrant, energetic, and young at heart. We are youthful.

We intentionally connect with each other to reach our aspirations of zen. We each manifest a tranquil essence based on principles of serene self-awareness. We strive to remain relaxed and composed while reflecting meditatively on our peaceful partnership. We are a calm and harmonious couple. We are zen-like.

We intentionally connect with each other
to reach all of our aspirations. Through the
shared reading and consistent application of
these Aspiring Affirmations, together,
we exemplify a truly special partnership.

We are: authentic, balanced, connected,
devoted, evolving, (best) friends, grateful,
honorable, intentional, joyful, kind, (in)
love, mindful, nurtured, open, (at) peace,
(of the highest) quality, respected, secure,
tender, united, validated, willing, exploring,
yielding, (full of) zest, attentive, beautiful,
calm, desired, (at) ease, forgiven, great,
happy, intimate, (on a) journey, kin, loyal,
motivated, natural, optimistic, patient, quiet,
rooted, supportive, trusted, uplifting, valued,
wise, (an ideal) example, youthful,
and zen-like. And So It Is!!

About the Author

Jill Guzman is a devoted and loving wife of almost twenty years, and with an undergraduate psychology specialty, a master's degree in gerontology, a social services career, and a variety of volunteering, she has always had a passion for both her marriage and helping others. Now retired with her husband, Alex, Jill is living her best life, with the love of her life, in Williamsburg, Virginia. The couple enjoys exploring the area with its history and beautiful nature, along with dancing and philanthropic giving.

To honor her parents, Jill and Alex have established a charitable fund through their local community foundation, to which a percentage of the proceeds from her books will be donated. Jill's mission is to diligently strive to live with intention, deepen her marital connection, experience and embody peace and joy, and, with humble gratitude, shine light into the world.

Leaving a review on Amazon or your point of purchase would be greatly appreciated. You are welcome to visit the author's website at jillguzman.com and feel free to reach out via email to contact@jillguzman.com. Thank you.

www.ingramcontent.com/pod-product-compliance
Lightning Source LLC
Chambersburg PA
CBHW040934030426
42337CB00001B/6